The Hundredth Nubian Effect

How to get ahead even if you
start from behind

LaTanja Watkins, MD

Printed in the United States of America

First Printing, 2018

ISBN: 978-1-7326463-0-8 (Paperback)

ISBN: 978-1-7326463-1-5 (Kindle)

Website: http://www.hundredthnubian.com

Facebook: The Hundredth Nubian Effect (@hundredthnubian)

Do you have something important to say?
Learn how to become a best-selling author in 90 days!
https://xe172.isrefer.com/go/curcust/latanja

I dedicate this book with gratitude to my first teachers who have loved, taught, and inspired me so that I may do the same for others:

Daddy
Mama
Coco (Boyce)
& Lawrence

If you would like to dive deeper into the concepts of this book and start getting ahead even faster, go to

www.hundredthnubian.com

to download your FREE workbook.

Contents

Introduction

I stand holding a human heart in my hand. As I glance down into the arteries and chambers, I wonder who was this? Who might he have been? Why is he here?

Forensic pathologists are some of the few people who have the opportunity to stare death in the eyes every day. One cannot enter into this field of medicine with a feeble mind or faintness of heart because we see the worst of the worst and we are privy to the most intimate details of the last moments of a person's life.

Every day, I evaluate and determine the cause and manner of death. Bearing witness to the last vestiges of life is extremely humbling. It is final; it is real; and it is finite.

I believe it to be one of the greatest gifts that I have been given because I have never been so grateful and excited to be alive and to make the most of my own days here on Earth. Reflecting over my experiences, I often wonder if the people who end up on my autopsy table ever had the privilege of fulfilling their purpose in life.

You see when I initially wrote this book, I was working in the city of Chicago, Illinois, which, as you may know, is a city that has one of the highest murder rates in the country and the majority of these deaths are from gun violence. A disproportionate number of these homicide victims are young African-Americans, mostly male. For me, it was extremely painful to consistently see the premature death of way too many African-Americans in this country. The ripple effect is far reaching. Families, communities, and even the world cry out as we watch lives cut short.

This issue is the big pink elephant sitting comfortably on the couch in the living room of our country. Hardly anyone is saying anything or acknowledging his presence, yet he is there. I think part of the reason why people are hesitant to discuss this polemic is that we don't know the answer to solve the problem; furthermore, some people just don't care unless it affects them. What they fail to realize is that this, indeed, affects everyone.

It is our burden to bear because every human being has the power to change the world; I believe that anything is possible and that there is a genius in everyone. Simply put, I believe that every human being has a purpose that cannot be fulfilled by anyone else in the universe. Although these beliefs are challenged every day, I still choose to believe them because they are true. But how can people who leave life too soon contribute to society and offer their gifts if they are no longer here?

The answer to this question is ripe with paradoxes. Right now, the entire world seems chaotic, out of control, and scary. However, I believe that our society is in a state of chaos and tragedy that could lead to tremendous growth and that could propel us to become a better society if we choose to accept the challenge. Yet, as with any growth spurt, there are going to be growing pains.

Currently, these growing pains are showing up in the black community as Trayvon Martin, Alton Sterling, Philando Castile, Sandra Bland, and what seems to be an endless list of other people of color, have unfairly had their lives cut short at the hands of a few police officers as well as people from their own communities. These growing pains continue to manifest in the unjust violence that is directed towards innocent police officers as retribution for the actions of a few in the black community.

As the daughter of a retired high-ranking police officer, this breaks my heart. I cannot even attempt to imagine *what if that had been my father, with so much character and love in his heart, who was killed while on duty* ? My father always taught and encouraged me to be both empathetic as well as a champion for justice. In addition, I continue to also see these growing pains on a daily basis in my work as a forensic pathologist and medical examiner. It makes me pause and ask, if not us then whom?

In her book, *The New Jim Crow,* Michelle Alexander makes the compelling argument that it *must be* us. Racism in America never ended but was rather redesigned. We have been taught all of our lives that the painful part of our history is over and that people have moved on, but, in actuality, it seems that the ugly beast of overt injustice, systemic inequality, and racial prejudice has just been lying dormant and striking so insidiously that he doesn't cause too much of a stir. He, like Bigfoot, enters and exits with very little fanfare. Sure, there have been a few reportings and sightings, but up until now there has been no definitive evidence that he is alive and thriving. Yet, the technology of our society and social media has caught up with him like a drone in the night, illuminating the fact that while we thought he had died with the American Civil Rights Movement, he is still very much alive and well. The spotlight shines on him, but we refuse to see it.

The question is now that we know that the Bigfoot of America clearly exists, what are we going to do about it? And in this very moment, we have a decision to make. In the midst of all the chaos, hurt, injustice, and pain, we have to decide exactly who it is that we are we deciding to become, both as a country and as individuals.

I ask you: Who are you becoming in this exact moment? Is it a person full of fear, anger, and despair? I know that is the initial reaction of many, if not most, but I don't think that this is the person that any of us came into this world to become. It certainly doesn't nurture the gifts that each of us has inside of us that we are meant to share and give to this world. In the end, we cannot allow fear and hatred to win this fight because you cannot fight hate with hate. The only way to conquer hate is with love. In order to come out victorious, you must fight adversity with triumph and you have to combat the feelings of despair with ones of determination. Believe that you will reach your destiny.

The Hundredth Nubian Effect

So what is the Hundredth Nubian Effect? The inspiration for this book came to me after hearing Dr. Wayne Dyer discuss a book by Ken Keyes called *The Hundredth Monkey* which illustrated events that took place when there was a shift in the collective conscious of Japanese snow monkeys who were observed in the wild for thirty years. According to the book, the monkeys were provided with sweet potatoes that were dropped off to them in the sand. Intended to serve as food, the sweet potatoes were delectable to the monkeys; conversely and understandably, they were not very fond of the taste of the dirt. Eventually, sick of eating the dirt, one of the monkeys came up with the idea of washing the sweet potatoes in a nearby stream and then she began to teach the other monkeys how to do it. They, then, taught more monkeys.

As the book explains:

> "Then something startling took place. In the autumn of 1958, a certain number of Koshima monkeys were washing sweet potatoes, however, the exact number is not known...Let us suppose that when the sun rose one morning there were 99 monkeys

on Koshima Island who had learned to wash their sweet potatoes. Let's further suppose that later that morning, the hundredth monkey learned to wash potatoes...Then it happened! By that evening almost everyone in the tribe was washing sweet potatoes before eating them. The added energy of this hundredth monkey somehow created an ideological breakthrough! But notice. A most surprising thing observed by these scientists was that the habit of washing sweet potatoes then jumped over the sea. Colonies of monkeys on other islands and the mainland troop of monkeys at Takasakiyama began washing their sweet potatoes. Thus, when a certain critical number achieves an awareness, this new awareness may be communicated from mind to mind...Although the exact number may vary, this Hundredth Monkey Phenomenon means that when only a limited number of people know of a new way, it may remain the conscious property of these people. But there is a point at which if only one more person tunes-in to a new awareness, a field is strengthened so that this awareness is picked up by almost everyone."

Some have argued that this book was based only on conjecture; however, testing a similar theory, Maharishi Mahesh Yogi discovered in 1960 that only 1% of a population practicing the Transcendental Meditation technique would produce measurable improvements in the quality of life for their entire population.

A paper published in 1976 showed the result of a 16% decrease in the crime rate of a certain community when only 1% of the population tested their theory of collective consciousness through meditation (for more on this topic see "Preventing crime through the maharishi effect" in the *Journal of Offender Rehabilitation*).

By now, you may be asking: What in the world do the actions of monkeys have to do with the work of a forensic pathologist and this book in particular? Reading and researching both of these stories had an extremely profound impact on me. I began to wonder what if these events were true and they are actually replicable? Imagine the changes we could see in the world!

I then wondered what would happen if a similar effect could possibly be implemented in the lives of the African-American community at a time when many of us so desperately need it. What if there was a blueprint that mapped out the foundations for individual success, communal fulfillment, and purpose in life? Then what if, as more and more people began to implement these principles, there was a certain critical mass effect that took place and we began to see a decrease in homicides, poverty, and destruction in our communities? Compounding this even further, what if we saw a measurable increase in purpose driven lives, strong family units, generational wealth, and intentional legacy building?

Like the monkey who realized that washing the sweet potatoes would not only benefit him, but others, it is my sincere wish for everyone who reads this book that we, collectively, will change the life trajectories of others.

What if there came a day when African-American youth (and adults) didn't have to question their inherent self-worth and true potential to not only make the world great but also their right to benefit from their contributions to this society? Our worth, dignity, and respect is equal to any other man or woman sharing the earth with us, regardless of ethnicity, class, or gender. Each of us has a gift that we were meant to share with the world, but our wounds and the wounds of our ancestors have had a dire impact on the way that we see ourselves and the world in which we live. What if we moved from harming and hurting to helping and healing?

My current line of work as a forensic pathologist and medical examiner has prompted me to question why my life looks drastically different from many of the young lives that are lost too soon to gun violence. As a medical doctor, I took an oath to "do no harm." It makes me contemplate what impacts a person's life so profoundly that they translate "do not harm" into "harm others."

Like many others, I was not born with the proverbial silver spoon in my mouth. Instead, when my parents had me, they were considered to be in the lower class financially. Yet, they managed to work their way through school and raise three children who have all turned out to be emotionally secure, purpose driven, and pretty accomplished academically.

Although they did not always have money, what they did have was invaluable and that was a plan for not only themselves, but for their children as well. At the end of the day, I believe this is what makes people who prosper in life different from those who do not. In the next chapters of this book, I lay out the blueprint for what I believe has made me not only a successful person, but also someone who possesses peace and fulfillment in my life. Regardless of what is happening in the world around me, I feel that one or more of these principles will always guide me back on the path to my personal purpose. The tenets of success that I live by and the directives that help me to fulfill my potential are ones that can assist and guide others if they are looking for a way out of their current circumstance or simply want to choose a different path in life.

Realistically, not everyone has someone in his/her life who has taught him/her anything of value in this respect and that is my purpose for writing this book. This certainly may not be the only way to achieve the life you want, but it has worked for me and I believe it will help others propel themselves to their full purpose and unlimited potential.

HEALING THE WOUNDED SPIRIT

Healing does not mean the damage never existed. It means the damage no longer controls our lives.
– Akshay Dubey

What Do We Do With a Cultureless Culture?

I have lost count of the number of bloody, non-beating hearts that I have literally held in my hands that belonged to black men and women who lost their lives prematurely to gun violence. Quite a few of them were, technically, considered children, younger than 21 years of age. I feel as though I have outlined about a gazillion wound paths of bullets. Searing through their skin, hearts, lungs, and brains, .38s, .45s, high velocity ammunition, and buckshots have each left footprints of destruction.

Black on black, white on black, police involved—it doesn't matter. All of them are heartbreaking to me and their loved ones; all of them impact every single one of us whether we would like to admit it or not. Each instance has left me exclaiming, WHAT IS GOING ON???

As I collect evidence and perform my examinations, I tend to think about things like why is this such a big problem in Chicago and other communities and what can I do to help?

Why don't members of other ethnic groups come into the office proportional to us? I can't help but to think that one, often unacknowledged, reason is that the African-American community has survived and adjusted to life in this country despite being totally stripped of their culture, regardless of whether it originated in Africa or even natively. This stripping of cultural identity was intentional and probably, along with unspeakable brutality, the only way that the enterprise of chattel slavery could be successful.

Men and women were stripped of their names, religion, and cultural practices. Men and women were stripped of their human status and regarded literally as animals and pets and often treated worse than the family dog. If people were allowed to have a marriage ceremony, it certainly was not honored as "Massa" had the right to rape a slave woman repeatedly, if not daily. Her own husband could not even protect her. The fabric of the family was ripped to threads and the vestigial effect was jolting.

Once slavery was over, the newly freed slaves were left to fend for themselves without any resources or land of their own and yet, despite the odds, many were successful. An example is the neighborhood of Greenwood in Tulsa, Oklahoma which was one of the most successful and wealthiest black communities in the United States during the early 1900s. It is often referred to as the "Black Wall Street." It was a prime example of cooperative economics amongst African-Americans. They built their own businesses and controlled their own economy. There were doctors, lawyers, and families who owned private planes. It has been said that one dollar would circulate within this neighborhood for up to a year.

However, against the backdrop of Tulsa's growth and prosperity, there were other forces that were growing in sheer strength and numbers. Unfortunately, a domestic terror attack led by the Ku Klux Klan in 1921 left the neighborhood in flames, with thousands of its residents murdered or rendered homeless. These were common occurrences during the late 19th and early 20th centuries when the newly freed slave population was essentially fending for themselves and trying to establish and reclaim a culture of their own.

This historical context is helpful for understanding why culture is critical to any group's success and advancement. Most people don't understand that history does not happen in a vacuum and thus, they ask why can't blacks make a way for themselves? They chirp, "Look at Jewish people, Asians, Africans, Italians, and others who were able to come over to this country, work hard, pull themselves up by their bootstraps, and live the American dream."

Yet, the truth is that we have and we still continue to pull ourselves up from our bootstraps, but people rarely ever consider that these other ethnic groups, in post-slavery America, have not endured what the descendants of slaves have had to endure in this country. Period. This is not to say that they have not endured anything because they certainly have. This is not to say that black people are the only ethnic/racial group that has had to endure being enslaved and treated inhumanely because that is not true either. Every ethnicity has been enslaved at one point or another, some treated just as awful as those in the Atlantic Slave Trade, but there has never to my knowledge been a form of slavery as egregious as chattel slavery was.

There is no denying that it is the decedents of black slaves in America that I am seeing in my office every day. Lifeless bodies riddled with bullets that lead to their loved ones on the news, protesting in the streets, and standing in the parking lot of my job in a state of despair. I would never wish this upon my worst enemy. How many children, young men, and women have to die before we realize their worth? How many great contributions to society have been lost forever because of their early departures?

I grieve daily for all of the potential greatness that is hemorrhaging from the black community. The same way that slavery eroded our cultural foundation, these deaths have changed the culture in black communities.

What cultural substance do we have to stand on as a foundation? This is what other ethnicities have that we don't. What mindsets are we instilling in our children? What are the building blocks that we give them in order to build their character? Are they being taught that the American dream is for everyone and being given the proper tools to pursue it? As they achieve success, do they know how to keep it, and most importantly, do they have a sense of legacy so that life will hopefully be easier for those who follow after them?

Black culture in America is like Humpty Dumpty 2.0. Our pre-slavery ancestors had a foundational wall of culture, embedded with esteem to stand on; we then experienced a fall, and now, we need everyone to come together and put the pieces back together.

Healing the Broken Pieces

Turn your wounds into wisdom.
– Oprah Winfrey

The Civil Rights Movement may have made people of color equal on paper, but it did not necessarily bring us equality in the hearts of all people nor did it promise anyone smooth sailing from thence forward. No signature of pen would predict or pre-emptively fix the damage of the past or present. The good news is that until you are broken, you don't know what you are made of.

The things that have been thrown towards our ancestors were effective to a certain extent, but I have reveled at the strength, beauty, creativity, and resilience that has been revealed in the remnants of the broken spirits, mentalities, and dreams of those who have come before us. One can't reside in the brokenness that comes with the past because broken people do not move forward.

Think about it this way: Have you ever seen a movie or a TV show where someone is trying to escape something in a car with no tires? While the idea is to get away really quickly, they are just inching along at what seems like a turtle's speed. There are sparks flying everywhere and all you hear is screeching that sounds like nails being slowly and methodically dragging across a chalkboard. That's what a broken person looks (and sounds) like trying to move forward in the world. The reality is that many of us have faced insurmountable obstacles and experienced deep and abiding pain and loss, but we must move forward and not get stuck in certain mentalities and mindsets that leave us feeling disempowered.

Getting stuck in feelings of disempowerment is counterproductive. In his book *The Power Paradox,* author Dacher Keltner links the outcome of these feelings to living in a state of chronic stress which further leads to the majority of the health problems that we see in our country. Furthermore, he makes the following observation: "Chronic threat and stress damage regions of the brain that are involved in planning and the pursuit of goals. The principle is clear: powerlessness undermines the individual's ability to contribute to society."

I feel like even people with the best of intentions will look at the current state of events in America and sympathize with another's feelings of anger, injustice, and hurt, but these feelings can also literally disarm you from unleashing your full potential. I say snap out of it! In order to break out of any situation, it is imperative that you know that you do indeed have the power to change it and you aren't restricted to using the lower energetic emotions of anger, hurt, and rage. When life seems to hurt the most, it is, ironically, the most opportune time to break free. It's hard at times to understand the *why* of things and the really raw emotions of anger and rage that accompany them, but healing needs to take place in order to step up, move forward, play big, and conquer any obstacles that you face.

I am by no means saying that you should ignore your emotions and feelings or that they are not valid—not at all. You have every right to feel anger and to feel outrage towards the injustices you see in the world. Life isn't a fairy tale or summer camp outing. Emotions are real and palpable. I understand that you may have endured some serious issues and circumstances in your life that have hurt you to the very core of your being.

What I am saying is to feel your anger and own it, but don't stop there! The next step is to then turn it into a productive anger or another emotion that you can use to fuel your energy towards pioneering or championing a cause rather than fighting against something. Otherwise, anger will consume you and keep you stuck exactly where you are or even worse, you will start moving backwards.

Imagine people you know who are always cantankerous, disagreeable or pessimistic. What usually happens is that these people end up living miserable existences consumed with anger on a daily basis and the person with whom they are angry with probably doesn't know or even care.

In other words, holding on to anger will not change anyone but you. It will keep you stuck and living in the past instead of focusing on your present and your future which are far more important. The people you are angry with will go on living their lives while you are consistently giving them, or whatever circumstance you are angry with, the power to determine how you live yours. It will dictate what you do every day, how good of a time you have with whom you choose to spend your time with, and simultaneously, block people, life experiences, and blessings from your life because the lens in which you see the world will be so distorted. This is unhealthy anger.

Healthy anger, on the other hand, turns into compassion for anyone, including yourself, who has been affected by a particular injustice or offense. It requires healing and forgiveness (not forgetfulness) so that you can be at your best in order to be a champion for everything that is the opposite of what you were so angry about. If your anger was fueled by injustice, it allows you to be a champion for justice. If it was fueled by child abuse, it allows you to be a champion to ensure that any child who comes into your presence feels nurtured and loved. The key to healthy compassionate anger, though, is that it requires healing and forgiveness.

Here is the thing, the world, as beautiful as it is can be, is also a complicated place besieged with negativity. The only thing that any of us can control is how we choose to respond to our circumstances. While healing and forgiveness are two words that many people do not want to hear and they find them hard to accept at times, they are usually the first steps in moving forward when you feel stuck in life.

If you are feeling trapped and in despair and you don't know why, especially when you have tried so hard to move from point A to point B, I encourage you to examine the areas where you may have unresolved feelings of anger. Anger is a powerful emotional energy and it can be used to destroy the things and life around you. Or you can channel it to build things up. The choice is entirely up to you and you will have to make the very critical life altering decision of whether you will choose to stay broken in a destructive space or move forward in your life, to heal, and to forgive.

Forgiveness

As I walked out the door toward the gate that would lead to my freedom, I knew if I didn't leave my bitterness and hatred behind, I'd still be in prison.
– Nelson Mandela

As some of you are pondering my words, you may be thinking: "Seriously? Why do I have to be the bigger person? Whoever and whatever my anger is directed toward certainly deserves to feel my wrath because I'm innocent and I did nothing to deserve this!" First, let me reassure you that I hear you; I see you; and I understand where you are coming from. Maybe you are feeling insignificant, unworthy, or even invisible right now. It can be overwhelming and exhausting, but we all reach this proverbial fork in the road at some point. It is not encountering the fork that matters, but the direction that we take and our rationale for why.

The most important question you can ask right now is what kind of life do I ultimately want for myself? If it includes fulfillment, success, abundance, connection, joy, or peace you have to learn forgiveness. It is a universal pathway to healing. I know forgiveness seems unfair on the surface, but in actuality, it can be one of the most selfish things in life that you can master. People just don't think of it in this way because the focal point is another person (or other people) and not yourself.

Forgiveness is for you. It frees you, not the person who wronged you. For the most part, they are already free unless something comes along their path that may cause them to have a change of heart and apologize. Holding on to the hurt and pain of the injustices of your past, of the past of our ancestors, or the past of your very own mistakes is the greatest form of self-bondage that we can subject ourselves to and it will keep you stuck and living in the past. It is akin to drinking poison. As illogical as it may seem, why would you drink poison to hurt someone else? Unforgiveness will significantly affect your inability to let things go, to move on, and to thrive.

Yes, forgiveness is hard and it seems unfair but, if you want to be a person who is limitless, it is necessary for your growth and advancement. Being consumed with anger takes an enormous amount of energy; the same energy, if transmuted, could be used to propel you closer to your dreams and goals. No one makes it through this life without being wronged in some way. Many people have had tragic experiences and are stuck with having to overcome them. I understand. In my own circle of family and close friends there have been issues with alcoholism, sexual abuse, and the unjustified murder of a child who did nothing to deserve it.

From personal experience, I understand what this pain looks and feels like. I was eight years old when my five-year-old cousin was brutally murdered by my aunt's boyfriend. It was a shock to our entire family, especially since we had only recently buried another aunt who had lost her life due to complications from Lupus. At the time, I understood that sometimes people could get sick or get to a certain age and go to heaven to be with God. I had no idea that bigger people could kill little people for crying too much. It was traumatic.

I was angry for a long time with the man who murdered my cousin and put her older brother in the hospital, but if I were still stuck there today, I believe my entire life would be different.

These things were hard to understand and emotionally damaging to me and to those I love, but I had to learn to forgive. Experiencing them at such a young age would affect my relationships with the men in my life and if I had not decided to use that energy for good, I would not be a medical doctor today. I can clearly remember vowing as a young kid that one day I would become a doctor so that I could comfort kids like my cousins and adults like my aunt and help them to not be in pain.

Realistically, no one will make it through this life without hurting or wronging another person. It has been said that "people who are hurting, often hurt others." Don't be that person who allows your anger and hurt to propel you to hurt other people. Keep in mind that the person or people who have hurt or betrayed you were most likely hurt by someone themselves. Furthermore, if you are not able to forgive others, you are very likely hurting other innocent people, including yourself.

I know this is something that is easier said than done and it also seems like it is the ultimate betrayal to yourself—just letting someone "off the hook" for their actions or inaction without any consequences. The thing about anger is that it is an emotion that lives in the past and if you are living in the past, you aren't able to move forward into your future. Whatever damage has been done to you, it lives in the past.

Just as with the pain that individuals experience, the damage that has been done to our people also lives in the past. Even if something happened two minutes ago, it is still in the past. This is now. I'm not intimating that certain things don't need to be acknowledged or addressed, but don't continue to carry hurtful events forward into your future in a way that will impede your own future growth, success, and purpose. At the end of the day, regardless of what is going on in the world, the only person who you have complete and total control over is yourself. The important thing to always remember is that the past is the past and it is impossible for the past and the future to exist at the same time.

Heaven and Hell Cannot Exist in the Same Space

Once you have started seeing the beauty of life, ugliness starts disappearing. If you start looking at life with joy, sadness starts disappearing. You cannot have heaven and hell together, you can have only one. It is your choice.
– Osho

This is one of my favorite quotes; I have it hanging in my office at eye level in front of my computer. It is a good reminder for me to focus on the good things in life since I see a lot of death and destruction every day. Kids are murdered, raped, and abused for no reason. I find myself reading the suicide notes that have been left behind from people who are so depressed and unsatisfied with their lives that they just decide to end it all. Life is ended in the blink of an eye for people who are just going about their daily activities and they just happen to be in the wrong place at the wrong time. The world is a crazy place and some of the people in it are even crazier!

I recall a time in medical school after my Psychiatry and Emergency Medicine rotations, that there was a period of time when I was really scared to meet new people. Based upon what I had experienced for those few months during those rotations, I was certain that there had to be more crazy and disturbed people in the world than normal ones. I barely felt safe enough to leave my house or even drive to work. I finally understood why, as a teenager, my father would not let me go places with my friends. While he trusted me, he did not trust the people "running about in the streets" as he called it.

Just like the protective parent, with the events going on in our society today, I can also understand why people are behaving in the ways that they are. If emotions are not properly dealt with and directed, randomly lashing out at other people is only to be expected. Also, for some reason, it is easier for some people to attach to the negative energy of life events than it the positive energy, even though the positive things are more prevalent. It is easy to forget that, in actuality, more people than not are actually really good people. At their core, just like most of us, they are just trying to live their lives as well as they can and provide for their families.

Additionally, throughout the course of our lives, if we are not careful, it is easy to get caught up in the agendas and the propaganda of others. While the stories you see in the media and across certain blogs are riveting and emotionally provoking, at the end of the day, their main agenda is to make money so the stories and headlines that you see will always be emotionally charged or divisive.

When it comes to social issues, the emotions elicited are usually fear, scarcity, injustice, hate, or rage. People and corporations invest significant monetary resources into marketing and copywriting that connects with you psychologically and emotionally using words. They can effectively and covertly push their political or monetary agenda. It is not necessarily salacious, but we should all attempt to be more aware of when someone is trying to manipulate or provoke us in order to push their own agenda. Otherwise, you will find yourself in a state of fear, hate, or rage more than you even realize. In turn, you become more susceptible to forgetting about the good in the world.

Think about it this way: If the news were your guide for understanding race relations, black families, and black children, what would you think? The black kids who are doing well in school, the good police officers in this nation, and the overall goodness and kindness of others would no longer encompass your worldview. By not guarding your emotions and thoughts, you are literally walking around in hell on earth, but you don't have to stay there.

You Are Allowed to Leave

No reason to stay is a great reason to go.
–Author unknown

At the end of the day, you are the author and creator of your individual life experiences. Therefore, you are allowed to leave any "story" that does not suit you. You are allowed to evolve and change at any point in your life for absolutely no reason at all. Just because someone tells you that you will never make it out of the *hood* because you are not smart enough doesn't mean that you have to believe him/her. Just because someone tells you that black women are unlovable and there is a scarcity of love and/or partners for them doesn't mean you have to buy into it and change your behavior in ways that ultimately devalue you. And just because the current propaganda is that the black community is inherently violent and we can't stop killing one another does not mean that we have to accept or believe that is our fate.

If I had listened to, and ingratiated myself into, every story and opinion that someone else had of me throughout my life, I would be in a very dark place right now, far away from my dreams, and I certainly would not be writing this book. Fortunately, I had parents and mentors who told me that the outcome of my life was up to me and that it would reflect the personal choices that I would make on a daily basis throughout the years. It troubles me when I see people value the opinions of others more than they value their own inherent self-worth and internal guidance. I don't care if Oprah, Beyoncé, Jay-Z, and the Obamas all show up on your doorstep tomorrow to tell you that you are unworthy, the only person who has the power to make that statement come true in life is you. You have control and hold *all* the power when it comes to *your* own life. Believe me when I tell you that whatever you dream of *is possible*. It certainly may not be easy, but waking up every day to a life that you are satisfied and fulfilled with is most definitely worth any sacrifice that you may make along the way.

One sacrifice may be the people who you surround yourself with. There will be other people who will try to keep you from bettering yourself or from writing the story that you desire for your life. Maybe you have decided that you don't want to struggle financially anymore, maybe you have decided to lose weight, or maybe you have decided to open yourself up to all of the many different and wonderful experiences and people that the world has to offer. Trust and believe me when I tell you that there is always someone there to say "no, you can't do that" or "who do you think you are?" More often than not, it is from someone who we admire and love dearly and whose thoughts and opinions actually matter to us. Many times, it isn't even intentional or malicious, but often when other people see you attempting to break free from your current circumstance, it makes them feel uncomfortable. It challenges them to reread and potentially change their own stories. They will tell you that you cannot accomplish something based off of their own inferior feelings about themselves. Yet, they will never admit that to you and many times, they haven't even acknowledged or admitted it to themselves. These people may be your close friends and family. Actually, most of the time they *will* be your close friends and family, but you are still allowed to leave any story that no longer suits you or supports wherever it is that you want to go. Do not let them stop you. Do not let them make you feel bad for wanting something different. Never be ashamed for wanting to experience life in all of its glory. You are meant to change. You are meant to grow. Keep moving forward and, if you must, let your mama, daddy, cousin Sally, or uncle Joe know that while you love them and always will, it's time to exit this old story so that you can create a new one.

You may be thinking that this sounds utopic. What about systemic racism and the social constructs that have been created to keep us in our place? Yep, you are still allowed to leave. While it may be more difficult for you than it is for other people, all you need is the right mindset, a solid plan of action, and the dedication and consistency needed to follow the plan through. Unless the boundary is planet Earth, as far as I know, you have the power to change it and even this boundary is debatable. The point is that whenever you have a choice to think big or think small, always thing big.

Don't Settle for a Small Life

If you keep telling the same sad and small story you will keep living the same sad and small life.
– Jean Houston

What is it that you would do if failure did not exist—if it were not even a possibility? I remember hearing a story about a farmer who found an egg and he placed it in his chicken coop so that it would be safe. The only problem is that he was unaware that the egg he had found was an eagle's egg and not a chicken's egg. The hen in the coop protected this egg as if it were her own and the egg eventually hatched along with the other chicken eggs in the coop.

The eagle grew up as a chicken and he mimicked the other chickens. The imprint was so indelible that when it went to fly, it would only fly as high as his fellow chickens did. It had no idea that it was an eagle.

One day, he looked in the sky and saw the grandest creature he had ever seen, an eagle. He was so in awe and got so excited that he proclaimed, "One day I, too, will be an eagle!" To which, the other chickens responded, "You're crazy! You can't be an eagle, you will always be a chicken."

The eagle then hung his head low and agreed, "You're right, what was I thinking? I could never be an eagle."

For the rest of its life, the eagle continued to live as a chicken. He never explored his true potential. He went to his grave thinking that he was a chicken.

How many times have you had a dream only to let external circumstances, or the opinions of other people, kill it? Have you had people tell you that it is not even possible to achieve your dreams? Many people are quick to give you opinions and advice on YOUR dreams based on THEIR own limitations. Don't let other people reduce your dreams to the level of their own expectations for themselves.

Let me tell you something: I don't believe God gives us a dream that is impossible to become a reality. It may take a little elbow grease and hustle, but I firmly and passionately believe that if I can dream something, then I can make it a reality. I just have to have a clear vision and every once in a while, my dreams may require me to think innovatively and to go against the status quo.

My life's story exemplifies the importance of dreaming. Even as a young child, there was no doubt in my mind that I would be a doctor when I grew up. I had a dream and something inside of me knew that it was possible for me. I remember very clearly when my friend's mother, the wife of a physician, told me that I should think of something else to do because physicians are really intelligent and since I wasn't on the honor roll at my school, I probably wasn't smart enough to be a doctor. I also remember very clearly, after demonstrating much hard work and discipline in high school and college, getting accepted into medical school in 1998 only to flunk out in 2000.

It was one of the most embarrassing and depressing times in my entire life, but I still had a dream and I knew that no matter what things looked like, it was not over. I also remember re-applying to medical school and talking with a prominent leader on the admissions committee at one of the historically black medical colleges. He told me that I should stop wasting everyone's time and apply to dental school or get a master's degree in public health because if there was one thing he knew, it was that I would NOT be enrolling in the next class of scholars at that particular medical school. I was devastated. I did my undergraduate studies at a historically black university which had been such a great source of strength and support for me.

I felt betrayed that someone, who was a leader at a historically black medical school, would be so discouraging. Had my belief in myself and faith in my dream been shakable then I possibly could have listened to these people who were, ostensibly, wiser and more powerful than me. I would not have persevered to go on to achieve my dream of graduating from medical school, let alone completing additional graduate training at the Mayo Clinic, one of the best medical institutions in the country.

There is something powerful about being steadfast and determined in regards to the dreams that you have for your life. Some people call it the law of attraction. Others call it God's will. My own life has shown me that whenever I get serious about pursuing something to the point that I will *not* take "no" for an answer, the world around me will begin to change in order to make those dreams come true. People will appear, out of nowhere, in order to help me. Others will appear in order to test me and fortify my dedication. Yet, as long as I am steadfast in my pursuit, success does eventually come.

Using my story as a template, don't let other people tell you what you can or cannot do. Don't live a life smaller than what you dream of because of the small minds and small thinking of other people. Don't live your life as a chicken when God created you to be an eagle! Dream big and set standards for what it is that you want out of the life that you have been given. If you want a life full of success, love, and abundance then live accordingly. Find the people who will support you. Be willing to do the various things that are needed to get you there. Life will meet you where you set your standards. Allow it to bring you the hope, circumstances, and people who will help to propel you towards your destiny and purpose. As Jim Rohn once said, "let others lead small lives, but *not you*."

Lay Your Burdens Down

Prejudice is a burden that confuses the past, threatens the future, and renders the present inaccessible.
– Maya Angelou

Prejudice isn't only wrong when it is directed towards you. It is WRONG. Period. I am beyond sick of people spreading the same principles of hate, racism, and prejudice that they are *so* indignant about having directed towards them. Bigotry is yet another thing that is not only inherently wrong, but it will also keep you from achieving your highest potential.

I think Martin Luther King Jr. said it perfectly, "Let no man pull you low enough to hate him." Remember, as I have stated previously, hurt people tend to hurt other people. Racism and prejudice are included in this. Unless you have the ability to create life out of thin air, then you have no right to feel anything less than love for any man or woman who has been given life by something greater than yourself. I often wonder why some people feel compelled to bring other people down in order to elevate themselves.

This seems to be particularly true in today's society. Yes, black is beautiful and I hope that every black person reading this book truly knows that in their heart of hearts. At the same time, I hope that we also understand that just because black is beautiful that doesn't make anyone else less beautiful. Black power doesn't mean that self-love is not important or relevant to other groups. Yet, I understand how our society's past (and present) has put us in the position that we need to reinforce beauty and empowerment both in ourselves and in our children. We have to work extra hard to instill in ourselves and our children the same level of self-esteem and security as other people in this society because we are not generally seen as the "standard" of beauty, intelligence, or even worth.

However, I sometimes wonder what the world would look like if we were to wake up tomorrow and the tables were turned. Is it possible that one day, we could wake up in a utopia where everyone loved each other as equals and all people were given the same opportunities? It isn't far-fetched to imagine a similar scenario as the one we see today (bigotry) only in reverse because bigotry is the result of ego and the illusion that you are better and separate from your fellow man. It makes you feel the need to feel superior to the person beside you based on your exaggerated opinion of yourself. It can be a problem in the heart of every man if it is not appropriately checked. Even a utopia can morph into a dystopia.

When applied within the construct of power, bigotry and prejudice have led to dangerous and destructive events such as the Atlantic Slave Trade, terrorism, and the Holocaust. As horrible as these events were to millions of people and as much as black people are still dealing with the effects of slavery to this day, it still does not give anyone the privilege of taking their anger and hurling it towards their fellow man in equally damaging and painful ways.

Do we envision that pain feels differently based on one's race, class, or gender? No, pain is pain. Perhaps it is a fable that can best illustrates why we must be mindful of how our actions affect others. "Burner Burnt," an Aesop fable, tells the story of a fox who had angered a farmer by doing damage to his crops. When the farmer caught the fox, he thought that he would make it pay severely for the damage it had done and the farmer tied a rope soaked in oil to the fox's tail and set it on fire. However, according to the fable, some god made the fox run into this same farmer's corn fields which were ready for reaping. All the farmer could do was run after the fox and lament over the loss of his harvest.

This story is a universal lesson in humanity and it serves as a warning against uncontrolled rage which can do serious harm to those who harbor it. The cycle of racism, hate, and prejudice must stop if you are to achieve your highest purpose and reach your destiny in life.

MINDSET

Keep your mind free of envy, and anger, and greed, and hatred, and jealousy, and revenge, and fear, because these are the seven dark riders of failure.
– **Napoleon Hill**

Accepting the Difficulty of Life

Life is difficult. This is a great truth, one of the greatest truths. It is a great truth because once we truly see this truth, we transcend it. Once we truly know that life is difficult— once we truly understand and accept it—then life is no longer difficult. Because once it is accepted, the fact that life is difficult no longer matters.
– M. Scott Peck

These are the opening lines from the book *The Road Less Traveled* by M. Scott Peck, a psychiatrist, who argued that life was never meant to be easy for any of us and it is essentially a series of problems which can either be solved or ignored. He believed that it is only because of these problems that we grow spiritually and mentally. Conversely, he hypothesized that the tendency to avoid our problems and the emotional suffering that tends to accompany them was the primary basis for much of the mental illness and personality disorders that he saw in his daily practice as a psychiatrist. From what I have seen in my own life and career, I tend to agree with this claim. People who tend to have problems in life usually have a sense of entitlement and the expectation that everything is supposed to be easy. It doesn't help that this viewpoint is consistently reinforced in the media and in our culture in general. You can accomplish any dream that you have set for yourself and attaining the life you want is simple, but it is rarely easy.

It is simple in the sense that if you can muster up the discipline, belief, and courage to follow the life principles outlined in this book, you will most likely achieve success. But it is *not* easy and the sooner that you realize this then the better you will be able to "cope" in life and continue on your journey towards success.

The difficulties experienced in life are what develops your character and your character is what gives you the strength to conquer whatever road that you choose to travel. Keep in mind that different roads require different levels of character. Character has been defined as the stable and distinctive qualities built into an individual's life which then determine his or her response, regardless of the circumstances.

Success or failure, in any situation, will depend on our character and how we choose to respond to the difficulties experienced in life. The sweet spot in life is figuring out how you can take the high road in any situation. That is the road to success and fulfillment. You won't always be able to control situations and you definitely are unable to control other people, but you can control your mindset, values, and how you choose to respond to whatever life throws your way. If you are bitter on the inside, you can't expect sweet mango juice to come out when the circumstances of life start to squeeze you.

The truth of the matter is that at the end of the day, what your life looks like is entirely up to you. We have been conditioned to think that external factors such as who are parents are or even who the current president is makes a difference as to whether or not we are able to make it in this world, but this is a misnomer. Some of us have also been conditioned to believe that it is the responsibility of other people or the government to make sure that we achieve success and happiness, but this is not true either because you and you alone are the one who gets to decide what your life will become.

No One Owes You Anything

You are responsible for your life. If you're sitting around waiting on somebody to save you, to fix you, to even help you, you are wasting your time. Only you have the power to move your life forward.
– Oprah Winfrey

That's right. No one owes you anything. Not. One. Darn. Thing. No one owes you a place to live or a chance to make it in life. The government owes you nothing. Neither do your family and friends. It sounds caustic, but the more you understand how important you are to your own destiny then the more powerful you are. You will no longer hide behind the shroud of being victimized when you feel like people have not given you what you feel they owe you.

Rather than feeling entitled, it is important to internalize that life and all of the things that you do have are a blessing. I'll bet that if you were asked to do so, you could sit here and come up with at least 10 blessings right now. Are you alive and breathing? Are you in decent health? Do you have clothes on your back? Shoes on your feet? A roof over your head? These are all blessings that should not be taken for granted. Furthermore, it is hard to make room in your life to receive bigger and better things if you are unable to appreciate the things that you currently do have.

In actuality, the only person who owes you anything is the one staring you back when you look in a mirror. Only you are responsible for giving yourself the life that you desire. Once you realize this, you move from complaining, wishing, and hoping into a space of creating. You become grateful for what you have and you make boss moves to get what you don't have. If you are in a miserable job, it's not your boss's responsibility to make it better for you. You have to do that for yourself. If you are in a relationship, the other person does not owe you happiness. You also have to do that for yourself. You owe it to yourself to change any circumstance that you are unhappy with. Learn a new skill or attach yourself to new people if you have to. Just don't wallow in resentment and wait for someone else to love or treat you the way you deserve to be loved or treated. Don't wait for other people to pay you what you are worth because you feel that they owe it to you. The reality is they do not owe you anything.

You Are the Master of Your Mind

Nothing will block your purpose in life more than a negative mindset. A pessimistic mind will never attract a positive life.
– LaTanja Watkins, MD

Regardless of what you are being told and shown on a daily basis, there is nothing inherently wrong with you. This is the biggest con in our society and droves of people fall for it every day. When you watch television, you get messages that you are inadequate because you aren't rich enough, aren't pretty enough, aren't thin enough, or aren't man enough. When you listen to music there's always a self-proclaimed bad bi**h telling you why you are less than a woman because you don't have a Gucci bag, red bottom shoes, or a boss boyfriend. Rappers spread the message that in order to be a man you need to have multiple bad bi**hes, an endless supply of money that you throw around at strip clubs, and a gun to kill anyone who dares to even look at you funny. Mind you, I like rap music as much as the next person and my goal here is not to censor or judge any form of artistry. However, there is power in words and even greater potency in images. That is why we see so many advertisements and sponsors choose shows that reach certain groups of people in order to sell them their products or to influence them. All kinds of knowledge is made available, but a person must be able to discern what will be beneficial or harmful.

I just wonder why it is that the black community seems to *internalize* these messages to the extent that we do. I see the internalization of these messages with the young people who I autopsy every day. I see some form of a rap song or hypersexualized, hypermaterialistic symbolism in their tattoo designs or on their clothing. Kids are losing their lives internalizing messages that are making some executive of a record, clothing, or production company beyond filthy rich. Take control of your mind! You can still enjoy whatever music or television show you like, but know that you don't have to co-opt the messages as your own. There are many more possibilities to life than what is being shown in your favorite music or television shows.

Also, you are not too _____ to do _____. Regardless of the words you use to complete this sentence, it's just not true. People are capable of doing almost anything that we set our minds to do, but most of us don't recognize or accept it. I'm not sure if it is because we never really take the time to think about it or if it is a result of the programming that we are bombarded with by our society every day. It's probably a lot of both. There are many corporations and people in this world who make money based off of our insecurities and lack of confidence in ourselves to achieve great things. Conforming to arbitrary limits and boundaries set by uninformed or misinformed people or institutions who do not have your best interests at heart is a way of life for most people because they have been programmed and coerced to think a certain way about themselves and what they are able to accomplish. There are some people who are not instructed on how to take responsibility for their own state of mind or beliefs. But one thing is for sure in this world and that is if you don't program your own mind, someone else will do it for you. If you don't take ownership of your dreams in life and what you want to do in this world, you will be destined to a life of building someone else's dream while yours withers away and dies.

Your mind, consisting of your views, ideas, and opinions of the world, is the most important thing that you have that must be protected from the control of others. Guard it closely and be aware of what you are programming it with because it can literally be the difference between life and death. If you program yourself with trivial matters, negativity, and nonsense that is usually what your life will reflect. However, if you make a conscious effort to program yourself with messages of empowerment, possibility, health, wealth, abundance, and love then these are the things that you will begin to see reflected back to you on a daily basis. The choice is yours.

Life Is About Choices

May your choices reflect your hopes, not your fears.
– Nelson Mandela

Life is about choices. This is the one piece of advice I heard over and over and over again from my parents, particularly my mother, while I was growing up. It was her favorite saying in the world. This was irritating to me because as a kid, and even as an adult, at times, I would often respond by saying, "Come on, surely I have no choice in this!" I remember one time telling my mom, "Come on, Mama. Now you know that I have to go to school. I absolutely have no choice."

Then, I remember her telling me, "No, you don't have to go to school. You definitely have a choice. You can go to school, or you cannot go to school. But one thing is for sure and that is that you have a choice, and when you make certain choices, you have to be prepared for the consequences of your choices. When you wake up every day and look around, everything you see is a direct consequence of every choice you've ever made. I want you to remember that you always have a choice, but with every choice comes a consequence. Even right now you can make the choice to not go to school, but you will suffer the consequences of whatever punishment me and your dad decide to give you, whether it be a whooping, or the juvenile detention center (they always threatened me with the juvenile detention center). You can also make any choice you wish as an adult, but be prepared to suffer the consequences of whatever that choice brings. If you don't go to school and limit your opportunities for a good career, you have to live with the consequences of possibly being poor and having to struggle every day of your life. However, if you do go to school and get a good career, you have to live with the consequences of possibly being prosperous and secure and being able to do whatever it is that you want. So, the choice is yours, choose wisely."

Reflecting back, I realize the potency and accuracy of my mother's words. As I write this book and I'm trying to figure out exactly what to say to those who read it, this is one of the most important thoughts that comes to mind: *We do all have a choice*. We do all face consequences. We can wake up in the morning and choose to have a good day or a bad day. When we are faced with various circumstances we can choose to see the bright side, or we can choose to see the negative side. When anything bad happens, you can choose to be the victim or the victor. We can choose to complain about life or be grateful. Life is all about choices. When you get to the heart of the matter, every situation is a choice. You choose how to react to situations. You choose how much other people will affect how you feel about your life. You choose to be in a good mood or a bad mood. It is worth stating again, your life, how you feel, and how you operate in the world is all based on the choices that you make from moment to moment and from day to day.

What choices are you making from day to day? What choices have you made in the last 10 minutes? When you turn on the television or listen to the radio, there are tons and tons of propaganda telling you who you should be in this world, but you have a choice. Truly ask yourself: Who am I choosing to be in this moment? Is it someone with a purpose? Is it someone with passion? Is it someone who can make a positive impact in the world? Am I someone who can commit to making positive choices every day, every hour, and every minute? I promise you that once you do this, nothing can ever hold you back from conquering the world, not even circumstances beyond your control.

Your Circumstances Don't Matter

Your present circumstances don't determine where you can go, they merely determine where you start.
– Nido Qubein

I'll be the first to admit that as African-Americans, we have been dealt some pretty crappy cards. Some of us are born into poverty. Many of us have not been born into poverty, but have been handed down generations and generations of a poverty mindset from our elders and those that have raised us. Some of us have never had to deal with poverty or a poverty mindset, but we still have to deal with institutional racism and being stereotyped by people who don't even know us; however, at the end of the day, none of these things matter when it comes to your potential for success. Your circumstances only mean the meaning that you assign to them, and if your state of mind is greater than what your circumstances currently are, your circumstances will change. They have no choice but to change.

Oprah Winfrey is a perfect example of this. One could argue that she is the most powerful woman on the planet. She had the most successful talk show for years; she is an actress who was even nominated for an Oscar; she has produced television shows and movies; and she is one of the biggest philanthropists on the face of the Earth. One would never know by looking at her that she was born in the deep south in the Jim Crow Era to an unwed teenage mother, or that she was sexually abused and became pregnant at the age of fourteen, or that most of the people in her early life and career told her that she would never be a successful talk show host. She was also told that she would never be an actress and she would never do great things.

I remember hearing her tell a story one time about a man she was dating who told her that he was the best that she would ever, ever get, and that she thought too highly of herself. I'm sure she and millions of other people thank God that she did not listen to him or believe that she was limited by the circumstances she was born into.

Think about this: What if she had internalized his words? Can you imagine? What if she actually listened? What if she actually thought that the circumstances of her life determined how far she could go or who she could become? While I'm sure it wasn't easy at all times, something in her soul stirred and said, "You know, this just is not true."

I'm asking you, are you willing to do the same? Are you willing to rise above whatever cards you have been dealt in life? Most of the time, circumstances are like mirrors and they constantly reflect what's going on inside of you, inside of your mind, and your heart. They are a reflection of you and what you are thinking. No one stands in front of a mirror with his/her hands to the side and asks, "Hey, why aren't you raising your right hand?" The raising of the hand comes from the conscious decision to raise your hand in the air. Similarly, as soon as you stop thinking about your negative circumstances and pointing out everything that is wrong in your life and you begin to make the conscious decisions to change whatever circumstances that you're unhappy with and how you view the world from the inside, then that's when your life begins to shift. The sooner you understand this, the sooner you can begin to change your world from the inside out. Focus your attention and efforts on the possibilities in life and not on the things that you are unsatisfied with.

✳✳✳

If you would like to dive deeper into the concepts of this book and start getting ahead even faster, go to www.hundredthnubian.com to download your FREE workbook.

Whatever You Give Your Attention to Is Guaranteed to Expand

Life is like a camera, just focus on what is important and you will get a great shot.
– Unknown

There is a saying that states that you always get *more of* what you focus on, and if you are focusing on the negative, don't be surprised when more negativity continues to show up in your life. Your life is a direct reflection of how you think. No, you can't control everything that happens to you in this life, but you can control how you think about your circumstances and how you respond to them.

Sure, these are nice things to say, but how can you apply them to your everyday life? In other words, what does all of this *really* mean? There is a quote by Dr. Martin Luther King, Jr that expresses this point exquisitely. He once said, "If you can't fly, run; if you can't run, walk; if you can't walk, crawl; but by all means keep moving."

If you're trying to get to a certain destination and the best way to get there is to fly but you can't fly, don't focus on the fact that you are unable to fly because you will never get there and all you will think about is not being able to fly.

On the other hand, if you stop focusing on the fact that you are unable to fly and, instead, focus on alternative ways that you may be able to get to your destination, you may realize that you may not be able to fly, but you do have a car so maybe you can drive. For those that don't have a car, you might realize that while you may not have a car, you do have money for a train ticket or bus ticket. You may even realize that you have a friend who has a car who would be willing to drive you. The point is that many of us get so caught up focusing on what we can't do or what we don't have that we lose sight of the destination all together. Don't be that person who is so focused on being poor that he forgets that what he really wants is abundance. Don't be that person who is so focused on being sick that he forgets that what he really wants is to feel good in his body. Don't be that person who is so focused on why she is single and why nobody on Earth adores her that she forgets that what she really wants is love and companionship. You have to focus on your final destination and what it is going to take to get you there. Don't let circumstances control you. Take control of your circumstances and move forward.

Your Attitude Will Determine Your Altitude

Impossible is just a big word thrown around by small men who find it easier to live in the world they've been given than to explore the power they have to change it. Impossible is not a fact. It's an opinion.
– Muhammad Ali

In the summer of 1991, I was accepted into the math and science for minority students (MS^2) program at Phillips Academy in Andover Massachusetts. That program changed the course of my entire life and for that, I will be forever grateful. You see, Phillips Academy is a very prestigious school, probably more prestigious than any of the students in the program realized at the time. It is a well-known and esteemed boarding school with alumni of the likes of Humphrey Bogart and Presidents George H. and George W. Bush. I remember getting to campus and one of the first things that I heard was, "Always remember, your attitude will determine your altitude in life." I didn't know the importance of these words at the time, but the people who ran the program and who would mentor me over the next three summers did. Not only were the alumni impressive, there were students from all over the world who had come to further their studies over the summer. Many of them were pretty well-off and brilliant which was, at first, intimidating.

The purpose of the program was to not only cultivate our interests in math and science but also to expose us to a world that many of us did not know existed. I believe the purpose of that motto was ingrained in us to the point that even though we came from underserved communities, we began to believe that anything we dreamed of in life was possible as long as we kept the right attitude. Everyone was taught to accept the concept that we could succeed. Complaining and lack of confidence were addressed and defeated by our mentors because they understood that these were dream killers. Negativity is like weeds growing in a garden. If you don't do what is necessary to remove the weeds then they will overtake your garden and destroy your crops.

Many people don't realize the bearing their attitudes have on their outcomes in life. Your attitude carries powerful energy that can either thrust you towards success or halt you in your tracks. Regardless of whatever difficulty you are challenged by, you are always in control of your attitude and how you respond to any situation. You have to decide whether or not you are going to be a warrior or a whiner. You have to decide whether or not you are going to be a champion or a chump. You have to be determined to keep a positive attitude even when you are in a job that you hate, a terrible relationship, or when people don't like you. It is the one key factor that will either push you forward or hold you back. Perspective is everything. What makes any event wonderful or tragic is your perspective and your reaction to the circumstances.

Gratitude

Let gratitude be the pillow upon which you kneel to say your nightly prayer.
– Maya Angelou

It is essential to realize that regardless of your life circumstances and regardless of what you have or what you don't have, in this moment, you are enough and you have enough. It is very important to be grateful for that. Gratitude and joy are two of the greatest forces on Earth that lead to change. The life of an ungrateful person is filled to the brim with dissatisfaction, frustration, and emptiness. When you can be truly thankful for every moment of your life up until now and the lessons they have taught you, you cannot help but to attract even greater levels of meaning and purpose in everything that you do.

Additionally, gratitude keeps us connected to the things that are working in our lives, rather than dwelling on the things that are not working. Take a second and sit quietly and think about everything you are grateful for in this very moment. Do you feel your mood change? Don't you feel better? Wouldn't it be wonderful if we could remember to feel this feeling of gratitude in every moment of every day?

We'd be so full of joy walking around with spirits uplifted. This is an immense contrast from how many of us are walking around with feelings of stress and overwhelming frustration. It's not necessarily easy, but I challenge you to make the shift from grouchiness to graciousness.

Instead of complaining about how things are, be grateful for what you have and focus on how to attract the things that you want. There is a reason why preachers tell you in church when praises go up, blessings come down. It's because when we give the energy of gratitude, we attract the same kind of energy back to us, which opens up an entirely new world of possibilities, opportunities, and change. A grateful outlook will allow you to turn any setback into a comeback.

Joy

The present moment is filled with joy and happiness. If you are attentive, you will see it.
– Thich Nhat Hanh

One of the most underestimated superpowers on the face of the earth is having a spirit of joy. Think about a healthy, newborn baby. What is one of the first things that indicates a live birth? The sound of joyful noise or the bellowing of a baby's cry.

We come into this world with joy, but where does it go? If you look at a baby, all you see is pure joy. Why is it when you look at the average adult you are more likely to see dejection more often than you see joy? Somewhere along the way it is lost. Commercialism and consumerism are often culprits in stealing our joy factor. Retrace your steps over the last 48 hours and think of the commercial program for at least one television show that you watched. Subconsciously, we are constantly being told that we do not have the right to be happy and joyful unless we have a certain pair of shoes or a certain brand of clothes. That you are not enough if your skin tone isn't pleasing to some random group of people or you are undesirable if you are not married, or you are not successful if you have not accomplished certain material comforts. It is sad that so many people fall prey to these ideas and walk around sad and depressed.

Stop waiting for something "good" to happen before you even consider being joyful about your life! Happiness ALWAYS happens NOW. It is a feeling and a state of being. It doesn't depend on anything external because it come from within. At any time, if you don't feel joyful NOW, it is because you are choosing not to. Joy is about you, not things or other people. It is about being comfortable in your own skin and taking advantage of the life that God has given you. Are you even aware that up to 65% of embryos do not even make it out of their mother's womb due to natural miscarriages? That is not even counting elective abortions! Regardless of whatever is going on around you, whether you drive a certain car, have a companion, or don't have any money, life is a gift and it should be treated as such.

This is especially poignant when you are surrounded by death. Every day at work, I come face to face with those of us who, for whatever reason, did not make it to see another day. The fact that you are even here to experience the convolutions of life is something to be joyful about. You are a miracle! Make up your mind to be joyful no matter what because when you count your blessings instead of focusing on what is lacking or wrong in your life, your blessings will multiply.

How are your thought patterns and behaviors undermining your joy? Do you expect things in general to go well or to be disastrous? When you think about your life, do you think about your failures more than you do your successes? The more you focus on the negative, the more you are unable to see all of the great things that are around you in abundance. Even on the worst day of your life, you can always find one thing to feel joyful about. Find that thing and hold on to it. Use it to carry you forward and away from negative thoughts.

Be Authentically You

Be who you really are. Often people attempt to live their lives backwards; they try to have more things or more money in order to do what they want so they will be happier. The way it actually works is the reverse. You must first be who you really are, then do what you need to do in order to have what you want.
– Margaret Young

Don't be afraid to be yourself. Many of the greatest men and women who have walked the Earth are eccentric and nonconformists. Look at Prince, Michael Jackson, or even Dr. Ben Carson (regardless of what you may think about his political opinions, he is one of the greatest physicians in the world and was a significant influence on many black physicians' decision to go into medicine). All of these men are unique and at different times in their lives, they did not fit into the crowd, but they are or were the greatest in their respective professions. In 2016, Issa Rae gave us pure television genius with her show "Insecure" on HBO. We never would have been able to enjoy the show if she were ashamed of being the "awkward black girl" that she is. Great men and women are not afraid to be themselves even if they are different.

It is important that you live your truth and be who God created you to be. There is a reason that we are all created differently. It is because we all have something special and unique to give to the world. It is impossible to be your best self and live up to your purpose when you are walking around constantly trying to be someone else. We spend way too much time and energy caring about what other people think. And guess what? It's none of your business. Not everyone is going to like you. Not everyone has to like you. And here's the thing—you can spend all of your time and energy trying to mold yourself into the perfect version of you for someone else only to realize that the next person doesn't like you. Where do you go from there? It's a vicious, nonproductive, cycle that impedes you from specifically doing what you came here to do and it dims your light.

You have to realize and acknowledge how special and unique your particular light is. If it is not shining, it is unable to attract your birthright to you—the people and opportunities that were created specifically for you. Your purpose in life will always elude you if you seek your validation and measurement of self-worth from other people and their opinions of you. Be yourself and the people who are supposed to like you will!

Don't live small so that other people can continue to be comfortable because you fit into their box. I, for example, am an introvert and I don't apologize for it anymore. Nothing makes me happier then to come home and take a long hot bath and read as many books or watch as many esoteric YouTube videos that I can fit into my brain. When I do go out with my friends and make time to be social, I don't do it anymore unless I have had my "me" time. Otherwise, I would go out and not be very good company because I would rather be at home and that doesn't make for a very good time for anyone. So now I am very upfront about this and my friends and family know that I need my down time. Regardless of anyone's personal opinions of whether or not

I should go out more, people tend to respect my honesty about who I am. Additionally, because I honor who I am, I can also honor my purpose, which includes being a conduit for my own personal growth, success, fulfillment, and transformation.

Excuses

Excuses are tools of incompetence which build monuments of nothing and those who specialize in them seldom accomplish anything.
– Author unknown

Any member of a Divine Nine Greek Organization has recited this, or some related version, ad nauseum and its value extends far beyond attaining three letters. If anyone on Earth is going to entertain your excuses, it's going to be your mama and hopefully not for long. The rest of the world does not care. They don't care why you couldn't make it on time or why you couldn't call them back. They just know you couldn't and that makes you incompetent. You have not lived up to what you said you were going to do; therefore, they will have difficulty putting their trust in you to get anything accomplished. It's that simple. Stop making excuses. They are meaningless and provide nothing of value.

I'm not saying that you will never have obstacles because we all have obstacles. However, we should all be active participants in the resolution for any struggle that may cause us to not keep our word. What excuses are you making? How are they keeping you from moving forward? Perhaps you frequently find yourself saying I don't have enough time when, in actuality, the problem is a lack of focus or discipline. It suggests that maybe you don't have your priorities straight or that you are lacking the discipline to bring things into fruition. Or maybe you just don't desire something as much as you say you do because people make time for what's important to them. There is always enough time. Therefore, if you desire something badly enough you may have to sacrifice the time that you are spending on something else.

Another popular excuse is "I am too young" or "I am too old" when, in actuality, men and women of all ages have achieved all sorts of spectacular things. Did you know that there are twice as many millionaire entrepreneurs over the age of 50 than there are ones in their 20s and 30s? This makes me wonder why people, especially women, start to feel as though life is over for them once they hit the age of 35 or 40. Lies! Do not fall into this trap and willingly dim your light before it has even had the chance to truly shine.

One of my favorite inspirations is the life of Ernestine Shepherd who is the oldest female bodybuilder in the world. She didn't even start working out until she was in her fifties. Today, she is in her eighties and not only is she beautiful, vibrant, and strong, but she looks like she's in her mid-forties. Every morning, she wakes up at 2:30 a.m. and sets out on a 10-mile run! She teaches fitness classes and inspires other senior citizens to exercise and take care of themselves. At the age of 40 or 50, she could have said "I'm too old" and prepared herself to succumb to the common health problems experienced by middle aged and senior citizens around the world like severe arthritis, immobility, and diabetes; instead, she chose to see her age as just a number and she chose not to make excuses for herself. This is exactly what all of us should do because at the end of the day, successful people succeed, and unsuccessful people have really great excuses as to why they cannot. Stop making excuses and start making changes.

Self-Worth

*Make sure you don't start seeing yourself
through the eyes of those who do not value
you. Know your worth even if they don't.*
– Dr. Thema Bryant-Davis

Self-worth is the opinion you have of yourself and your value. In our society of extreme consumerism, many of us have been brainwashed into thinking that this value comes from external sources. If you don't have a Louis Vuitton bag, expensive clothes, or a voluptuous back side, you are not valued as a woman. If you don't have an expensive car, a six-figure job, or plenty of bad bi**hes, you are not valued as a man. While I've never been ashamed of being black, there is one time that stands out in my mind where I was embarrassed by a seemingly popular mentality within our culture.

In 2012, we had the pleasure of being witness to Gabrielle Douglas who was one of the very few black gymnasts who has ever made it to the Olympic Games and she killed it by being the *first* black woman to take home the gold medal in the All Around Individual competition. In that moment, I was so proud of her and I was really proud that she served as an international symbol for young black women. In the next moment, I was almost in tears because on social media all I kept seeing was feedback from other black women that her ponytail was not up to par by their standards. I was sick to my stomach. I just couldn't figure out why people would go out of their way to drag this young lady down over something so foolish and, by the way, natural. We then had a repeat of these foolish shenanigans in 2016.

It doesn't stop with Gabrielle Douglas's hair. Unfortunately, you see it everywhere. Oprah Winfrey has become practically Superwoman on Earth, but some people always feel the need to point out that she is overweight or unmarried. Sean Carter (Jay-Z) has become one of the most brilliant businessmen and arguably the greatest rapper of all time, but some people always feel the need to point out his facial features as if it will magically make him unworthy of his accomplishments of being one of the greatest rappers ever and an extremely successful businessman, or less attractive in the eyes of his wife. Not that he even cares how you see him. He might as well have dropped the microphone when he rapped some of the truest words ever spoken to his haters "I'm a billionaire, I'm cute." The thing is, what you criticize in others is really a reflection of where you gather your own self-worth. It is a symptom of people who consistently look outside of themselves for validation and a sense of their value and who also tend to give uninvited criticism to other people. Those who are criticizing are typically not doing much of anything except disparaging other people. In fact, in the grand scheme of life, I would bet that they are nowhere near accomplishing much of anything.

Stop it. It doesn't affect the achievements of the people you are criticizing because in order to get to where they are, they usually already have their self-worth in check. Tearing others down will not make you any more successful, beautiful, or worthy. People who operate and live in this state probably won't be the first to do anything, or even accomplish anything great for that matter. In order to accomplish anything, you have to believe that you are valuable enough to receive it. You have to believe that you are worthy. I believe that you can get a sense of your own self- worth by taking a look at how often you criticize others and what you criticize them for. There is more to you than your back side or your income. There is more to her than her hair and her clothes. There is more to him then how much he makes or what he drives. Most importantly, there is more to you than what you are criticizing others for. Trust me when I tell you that what you put others down for is more of a reflection of you and how you value yourself.

On the other side of the coin, there are people who are unable to receive compliments because they feel unworthy on some level. You can tell someone she looks nice and she will argue that she doesn't. You can tell him that he is gifted and he will argue that he is just like everyone else. They are super determined to be less than who they are. If you do this, stop it. This doesn't serve anyone, not even yourself.

Friends

You are the average of the five people you spend the most time with.
– Jim *Rohn*

Let's talk about friends, shall we? The people who you choose to confide in and spend the majority of your time with will be the most important decisions that you will make in your life! I feel so strongly about this statement that if I had to choose only one lesson that I could teach the world on how to achieve ultimate success, it would be this one. We are greatly influenced by the people who we spend our time with so the people you have around you matter. You want to surround yourself with people who have dreams just as big as yours or even bigger than yours. You want to have friends who can challenge you, make you better as a person, and reprimand you when you are making excuses for yourself. And when you are trying to reach a particular goal in your life, the people who you spend the *most* time with should have very similar goals.

Like many, I learned this principle experientially. I remember my freshman year of college. I had worked hard in high school and my ACT scores put me in the position of earning a full scholarship. I had chosen one of my best friends from high school, who had also went to Phillips Academy with me over the past three summers, as my roommate so that I wouldn't get into too much trouble. She was studying to be an engineer and I wanted to be a doctor. Today, she is an engineer and I am a doctor. I say that I wanted to stay out of trouble because I knew enough about myself at the time to know that while I was smart and knew how to work hard, there was a part of me that wanted to, and often chose to, play first. I knew that in order for me to stay on track, I would need someone in my corner to hold me accountable and push me to be all that I could be. I chose the school that I attended because of her and her track record of being a true friend in my life who would tell me the truth with love whenever I messed up.

When I got to college, I pretty much had the time of my life during my first semester. I mean I had fun! I did my work and everything as well, but when my report card came out, I was disappointed in myself because I knew I could do better. And although I achieved a 3.0 gpa my first semester, I knew I had to do better in order to get into medical school if that was what I wanted to do. The two most heartbreaking grades I received were a B- in Algebra (because I had just aced AP calculus in high school) and a C in Introduction to Art because, well, it was Introduction to Art. It wasn't a hard class and I was just being lazy.

Early in the next semester, a dear friend came by my dormitory room to ask for help on some pre-calculus homework. Math didn't come as natural to her as it did to me, but she had received an A in Algebra because of her work ethic and determination. I learned about her willingness to sacrifice when I asked her if she was going to some party that we had planned to attend. She promptly responded, "Shoot, I don't have time for that mess. I need to get a grip on this math homework. I want to go to med school and be an ob/gyn and I'm not going to get there by partying. I need a good gpa." From that day on, she was my other best friend. The conviction in her voice and her actions illustrated that she would make it and do exactly what she had set out to do. I wanted to be right there with her doing what I had also set out to do.

It is because of her influence that I was able to do what I needed to do in order to get accepted into medical school with a 3.7 gpa by the time I finished college. And if you ask me (although I do have a very strong personal bias), she is currently the best obstetrics and gynecology medical doctor in the world. These two women are still two of my dearest friends in life in addition to the others that I have picked up along the way who also have strong work ethics and the ability to sacrifice the mundane for what it is they want to achieve in life.

The point is that if your friends are not going where you would like to go, doing what you want to do, or making as much money as you want to make (if this is your goal), it's time to find new friends. You may have wonderful people in your life right now and I'm not saying you have to kick them to the curb, but I am saying that the people you spend the majority of your time with should be in alignment with your goals and your vision for your life. If you don't currently know anyone, reach out to people online, join a meet up group, or even start one yourself, but it is imperative to find someone, or a few someones, as soon as you possibly can. The old adage is true, "Birds of a feather flock together." Find like-minded and spirited people who will help you accomplish your goals and catch your dreams.

Develop a Generative Mindset

There is always a way if you are committed.
– Anthony Robbins

Usually our first instinct is to rationalize why something we want to do will not work. You may want to start a business, but rationalize that you don't have the time. You may want to lose weight, but rationalize that you just have bad genes. You may want to travel, but rationalize that you just don't have the money. These are all convenient ways that we silence our inner greatness. In other words, if something is on your heart, there is a way. There is *always* a way if you want something badly enough!

I usually use these rationalizations to gauge exactly how much I want something to come to fruition because I know that with the things that I have genuinely wanted in this life, I have always found a way to make them happen. *No* was simply not an option and my fears practically became non-existent. This is what having a generative mindset looks like. You operate from a place where 'come hell or high water' you will find a way to generate the time, money, confidence, attitude, or people in order to get what you want.

A person with a generative mindset always sees an opportunity even in the midst of their obstacles. If they need an extra $3000 this month for something that will absolutely push them toward their goals like a coach or a class, they don't just say, "Oh well, I don't have the money". Their number one question, regardless of what their bank account looks like, is: "HOW in the world can I get this money? Maybe I could sell something or maybe I can get a part time job or maybe I can ask someone to help me"

The opposite of this is what I like to call an infertile and fruitless mindset because either you abort your dreams and goals before even trying or you try but don't give yourself an environment that will allow them to come to fruition or to grow and thrive. Either way, you only end up with what you had to start with which is nothing at all. The problem is that most people are not even aware of what mindset they are operating in each day. If you are unsure, begin to take note of everyday occurrences and how you respond to them.

Instead of automatically responding that you don't have time, ask: How can you make time even if it's only two minutes to start? Two minutes doesn't seem like much, but once you find two minutes, it won't be long until you can find four, then eight, then twenty, then forty, and so on. This may sound a little unorthodox, but you need to become obsessed with the things that you want in life like an addict who loves an illicit substance so much that he will go to the ends of the earth in order to obtain it and guard it heavily once it is acquired. I know this because I have found crack rocks hidden in the most painful and unbelievable places on people. God rest their souls.

Find and Pursue Your Purpose

When you realize God's purpose for your life is not just about you, he will use you in a mighty way.
– Dr. Tony Evans

Purpose is one of those esoteric words that people don't fully grasp, but they know they have one. It essentially boils down to what is it that you are here to do and it can be really overwhelming to think about. How does anyone know specifically what their purpose is anyway? Essentially when people are wondering what their purpose is, they are specifically asking what is it that will make their individual life important or significant?

Life is a journey and in it, we will find ourselves on many different roads. Purpose, figuratively, serves as the different stops that you make along the way. Collectively, these stops tell the story of your journey—what you did, what you learned and what you were able to teach to those who you helped. Most importantly, our purpose is linked to the gifts you give to the world along the way.

One of the easiest ways we can be sure that we are living in our purpose is being really attuned to the present moment.

And as you make the intention to be and do what gives your life the feeling of importance and significance each and every day, your gifts will begin to reveal themselves to you. You will find that by using these gifts and opportunities to serve others in your daily moments, you will be led down new roads with new gifts that will allow you to serve in even bigger ways.

Don't worry if you are not able to see the end result right away. I don't know of anyone who can. People may have visions of what they ultimately want to do in life, but using that as your end goal not only limits you, but it limits God, the universe, or whatever terminology you use to describe the unseen force in the world that is bigger than all of us. So, if you do have a vision for your life, hold it until you get there, but be open to bigger and better things that you may not be able to currently see.

The Expectation of Success

Whatever you expect, you will get. So expect success, not regret.
— **Dr. Debasish Mridha**

Successful people expect to succeed no matter what, and that expectation helps them to attain it. Achieving your goals is a faith walk. Hoping or wishing for anything in life will not get you very far without adding work. When you only hope for something you are basically saying that you are okay if it doesn't work out in the end. Hey, at least you tried, right?

Wrong. People go to school and hope that they get *straight As* only to end up with less. People get married hoping for a lifetime of happiness and end up divorced some years later. We hope for a lot of things. While hope is a good place to start, it is not enough. You have to add work.

When you add dedication and perseverance to your hope then it becomes an expectation and this is what breeds success. Your expectations affect how you show up in the world, interact with other people, and your willingness to take the actions required for you to get from point A to point B. If you expect things to go well, they usually will.

Likewise, if you expect things to end tragically, they usually will. If you only hope for things to happen, you usually end up somewhere in the middle.

When you set big goals, there will be resistance and even some emotional pain that you will encounter 100% of the time. The limits of your intellect, emotions, and ability will be tested. There will be things and people who you will have to sacrifice in order to move forward. Overcoming these things requires much more than hope.

You have to anticipate them, prepare for them, and fully expect to overcome them in order to reach the finish line because you will never be more successful than you think you can be. You can't play the victim when these things happen. They happen to others with worthwhile goals in life and nobody is immune or exempt.

Crying or whining about everything that is happening to you won't do you any good. Other successful people will just be like "Hey, join the club. Now what is your plan?" I once heard Dr. Wayne Dyer say that successful people don't think of things happening to them but rather about why these things are happening FOR them because you can't teach others what you do not know.

Regardless of the trials you may face along the way or the opinions that other people may have about your goals, you have to make the commitment to go for what you want and act with the confidence of someone who cannot fail. Things will go wrong, but you have to get keep going. When you fall, get back up. All successful people do. The one thing successful people have in common is that ALL have failed. A lot. But the failures did not prevent them from working on their goals.

Success Is a System, not a Secret

There are no secrets to success. It is the result of preparation, hard work, and learning from failure.
– Colin Powell

There is no secret to success. Success is all about having a system for applying common principles to your life. It is not rocket science, but it is more like a recipe for baking a cake or making a delicious entree. You simply have to have the ingredients of discipline, commitment, and persistence, a willingness to perform fundamental tasks, a willingness to sacrifice the lesser for the greater, and the aptitude to apply basic principles over and over again until you get the result that you want.

It is far from glamorous and it certainly isn't always fun, but the world will reward you for the execution of your ideas and not for your dreams alone. Your success won't happen in exactly the same way as your role models' success. More than likely, it will have the same underlying themes of discipline, commitment, sacrifice, and persistence. Success comes to those who are willing to grind it out day after day and keep their eyes on the ball even when excitement and passion fade into the background or go away altogether and morph into frustration and disappointment.

An additional attribute that I have noticed about successful people is that they are more than willing to invest in themselves in order to improve their skills. They will participate in masterminds, hire life and career coaches, take courses, and attend relevant workshops in order to get themselves to the next level. They don't care what anyone else has to say or think about it either. They know that self-investments are the best investments that you can make because they give you a platform to develop your gifts so that you can serve others better.

Most people believe that there is no reason to learn anything new after they complete their education, but if you want to achieve success, you must always continue to grow. I recently read an article that stated that the average American reads only two non-fiction books once they have finished school. If that statement is true, then I feel sorrow for the future of our country. Compare this to Bill Gates who, as reported by *Business Insider*, reads approximately 50 books per year and yet people will wonder how it is that he got to be so lucky. This doesn't sound much like luck to me. I think the better question would be: How did he become so driven, purposeful, ambitious, and inquiring? All of these qualities have contributed to his success more than luck.

Like Bill Gates and others, I thrive to learn more. Even with a terminal degree and board certifications, I see education as a life-long process. I often ask myself: How can I implement this strategy into my own life and self-motivated learning? I find that the cheapest and easiest way to implement this—if you want to be inspired or learn new skills—is by listening to podcasts. There are literally millions of podcasts that are readily available and they are free. You can find a podcast on nearly every subject your brain can think of and if you can't, then you should be the one to create it. MIT and Khan Academy offer courses online for free. Udemy is a great place to get plenty of courses for under $20. There is literally no excuse for not investing in your personal and professional growth.

Listening to a podcast the other day, I heard someone say that your income is directly correlated to how much you invest towards your own personal development. I'm not sure where they got this from, but it totally makes sense to me. Develop and follow a system that includes discipline, commitment, persistence, sacrifice, and self-investment and you are sure to find success and your destiny along the way.

You Are a CEO Whether You Know It or Not

Evaluate the people in your life; then promote, demote, or terminate. You are the CEO of your life.
– Unknown

Many people are on the bandwagon of being an entrepreneur and they feel that the only way to be truly empowered is to work for oneself. This isn't always practical for all professions though. It's hard to be an entrepreneur firefighter or brain surgeon for example.

The important thing to realize is that regardless of your occupation, you are the Chief Executive Officer (CEO) of your life and even if you work for someone else, you have to think of yourself as a business and an empire in and of itself. You have total responsibility over your own wealth and satisfaction in life.

A CEO is responsible for determining the direction and purpose of an organization; in this case, that is you. Your destiny does not reside in the hands of your employer, your spouse, your children, or the stock market. You are responsible for making the executive decisions in your life and recruiting your own board of directors (mentors and friends) who will support you on your journey. Furthermore, this means that you are responsible for educating yourself so that you are informed on the best practices available to accomplish your stated goals.

The average S&P 500 CEO makes 12.4 million dollars which is 335 times the amount of the average worker. I know a lot of people have strong opinions on these numbers and they think that they are unfair. However, these same CEOs also usually read an average of 50 books per year (remember Bill Gates) and they are no longer even in school! Yet, they still take the time to read an average of one hour per day first thing in the morning. Is it still unfair?

For reference, a doctorate and/or Ph.D. thesis is based on an average of reading and studying approximately 50 books which means that industry leaders, like Gates, are theoretically educating themselves to the tune of one Ph.D. per year. No wonder they make so much money! Most of us don't read further than Facebook and Instagram once we are done with school so I don't see why people have such a problem with other people's wallets when they have put in the work and have made sacrifices that others are unwilling to make.

Someone with a CEO mindset over his/her own life would aim to make S&P 500 CEO decisions on an individual scale in order to increase his/her own levels of success, abundance, and satisfaction. In order to be the boss and to live a boss' life, you have to be willing to pay the costs that bosses pay. What are you willing to sacrifice for the life and the success that you would like to have? Yeah, sometimes it sucks when everyone else is partying, but you have to stay in and work on your goals. However, one thing I have learned is that the pain of discipline is much more palatable than the pain of regret and disappointment. The dream is free, but the hustle is sold separately.

Closed Mouths Don't Get Fed

Ask for what you want and be prepared to get it.
– Maya Angelou

In all of my years, I have never met a mind-reader. You have to speak up for what you want. If you don't ask for what you want in life, the chances are that you are not going to get it. Not asking for what you want usually leads to a place where you find yourself feeling extremely overwhelmed and frustrated. People miss so many opportunities in life because they are too afraid to just ask for what they want or they automatically assume that other people should know what they want so they shouldn't have to ask.

This is the furthest thing from the truth. No one knows exactly what you want except for you so learning the art of asking for what you want is one of the best gifts that you can give to yourself. You can be hard-working and the best at what you do while being underpaid because you never had the courage to ask for a raise. You and your spouse can be perfect for one another yet still find yourselves frustrated in your relationship because you are afraid to ask for what you want.

Can speaking up be scary? Yes, it can be absolutely terrifying. Most people are afraid to ask for things because they are afraid of the possibility of being rejected, but you can't just sit back wishing and hoping that things get better or that what you want will fall into your lap. Miracles do happen some of the time, but the reason that a miracle is a miracle is because it is rare. There will also be times when you don't receive the answer or response that you want, but it should never be because you were too afraid to ask. Failing to ask ensures that the answer will be *no* 100% of the time.

Take Action NOW

Take action! An inch of movement will bring you closer to your goals than a mile of intention.
– Dr. Steve Maraboli

While education used to be the great equalizer between the haves and the have- nots, I believe that moving forward, distinctions will be made between the massive action takers and the mediocre people who are distracted and stuck in inertia. Because of technology, you have people out here who are literally making over 7 figures per year who did not even graduate from high school. There is no excuse for anyone to not dream bigger.

However, when doors open for you in this world, you better believe that there is plenty of hard work and hustle on the other side of them. The open door is only the beginning of the journey. You have to be a doer and not a wisher. People like to look at other people who have achieved massive success and say, "Oh, you're so lucky! If I had your luck I would be happy and rich too." Stop it with that nonsense! No successful person is ever "lucky." They have worked tirelessly to get where they are. Typically, they have done the work that the person calling them "lucky" was unwilling to do.

So how does one make this shift? A recommended first step that you can take is to actually write your goals down on paper. You can use something electronic if you wish, but I believe that something magical happens when you actually put pen to paper. People who write their goals down are actually 80% more likely to achieve their goals than someone who just thinks about them all day.

Once you have your goals written down, start to take immediate action on something. The only way you will learn what works and what doesn't is by taking action, doing something, or calling someone to ask for advice. As we have already discussed, there will be detours along the way, but as my mama would always (and still does) tell me when I got frustrated along my path: "It may be a long road, but just keep on walking. You will get there eventually."

Don't worry so much about what is ten, five, or even one year down the road. What can you do this month, this week, today, or even this very minute? Simply mulling over whatever it is that you want to do without any action is a sure-fire way to abort your dreams and you will only have yourself to blame for that.

Mentorship

You can't afford close association with people who are not vibrating on all 12 cylinders. Pick out the winners. Associate with winners because they'll do something to you. If you associate with failures, they will do something to you in spite of all you can do.
– Napoleon Hill

In addition to taking account of the five people that you currently surround yourself with, I encourage you to take account of the five people you currently go to for advice. Are they qualified to help you accomplish your goals? If not, you need to find new mentors to surround yourself with; search out mentors who've already accomplished what you're reaching for.

If I am trying to accomplish a new goal, I make sure to ask people that already know the answers as to how to get there. If your current mentors are not qualified to get you where you need to go, you need to find mentors who are. If you currently do not personally know a mentor who is successful at what you're trying to do then consider hiring a coach. If you do not have the money for a coach, you can find people on free podcasts or YouTube who offer plenty of free content that you can use until you have one or more mentors who you know personally that you could seek out for advice.

My brothers are entrepreneurs and before I set out to become an entrepreneur myself, I would hang around them and their friends and wonder why all they talked about was business and what they were doing in their businesses and I totally didn't get it. It was probably because my focus was getting through medical school successfully. My circle of friends and I talked about how we were going to matriculate through medical school and my brothers probably didn't get that.

In hindsight, I understand what both of our circles were doing. Iron sharpens iron. Someone with a degree in criminal justice is not going to be able to guide you through the challenges of medical school. Likewise, someone with a professional degree is not going to be able to guide you through becoming a six or seven figure entrepreneur within a certain time frame unless they have actually done it.

Find people who have done what it is that you want to do and send them an email or invite them out to lunch (on you) so that you can pick their brains and make a plan for yourself. Ask them how you can be of service to them. Even better, already have something in mind that you can offer them in exchange for their time and advice. Some people may say no or even be discouraging, but don't be afraid. He/she is simply not your person and that's okay. There is someone else who is your person and he/she is more than willing to help you. You just may have to experience a no or two in order to find the *right* mentor, but realize that any rejection is merely a difference of opinion.

Haters

Haters are like crickets. They make a lot of noise. You can hear them, but you cannot see them...and when you walk right by them, they suddenly get quiet.
– Unknown

Essentially there are three types of people: the ones who believe in you and support you, the ones who are indifferent and may need some convincing, and the ones who just straight up hate on you. Anyone who is trying to do anything great or of substance can expect to have haters. It comes with the job.

The urban dictionary accurately defines the word hater as, "A person that simply cannot be happy for another person's success. So rather than be happy they make a point of exposing a flaw in that person. Hating, the result of being a hater, is not exactly jealousy. The hater doesn't really want to be the person he or she hates, rather the hater wants to knock someone else down a notch." Haters hate because you are doing what they are unwilling or cannot do. Don't let it stop you. Never allow someone else's negativity to obscure your success.

Popular culture is fertile with examples of people who hate and are hated upon. One of the things that has always baffled me is why do people hate Beyoncé so much? She's pretty, brilliant, and one of the hardest working women in show business. Obviously, I am a fan, but no one can deny her talent or her work ethic. Yet people hate her. Because I am a fan, I always ask people why they hate her so much and I have yet to find a single person who can give me one legitimate reason. It's always something like I just think she is annoying or why should she be the star when the other girls were just as talented? Or she is just so full of herself. This response I really love because it always makes me laugh. I'm like "Who else should she be full of? You?"

I usually point out the fact that anyone who has the same determination, talent, and, work ethic has the same opportunity to be where she is. So why hate a person who has worked hard and sacrificed for her position when you or anyone else can do the same thing? Why hate a person for shining as bright as she can? Why should she dim her shine for you or anyone else? This goes for you as well. Never let anyone make you feel bad for living in alignment with your talents and your purpose in life.

On the flip side, when you find yourself hating on someone else, also remember that when you resent the success of other people, you also keep away your own success. What has been done for others can easily be done for you, especially if you are willing to do the work and make similar sacrifices.

The best way to fend off haters is to be discrete about your plans. Don't be braggadocios because everyone does not share your same excitement for your vision. Also, only confide in people who you know will support you and if they show any signs of being a hater, kick them out of your circle of trust immediately.

Discernment

Discernment is not knowing the difference between right and wrong. It is knowing the difference between right and almost right.
– C. H. Spurgeon

In previous chapters, we discussed that not only does the world not revolve around you, but everyone doesn't have to like you either. Once you get that lesson down then you should also realize that people who appear to like you and help you are not always what they seem and you have to develop your skills of discernment.

My father likes to tell me a story whenever I feel wronged or slighted in life. He says it is an Aesop fable, but I think it is a few fables put together with a couple of curse words thrown in for effect (although they will be censored for this book).

There was once a bird who fell from a tree into a ditch and in the process, it broke its wing. It could no longer fly and was stuck so it began to call for help. There was a cow who heard the bird calling out from the ditch and because he did not have the ability to go down into the ditch and rescue the bird, he did a #2 on him to keep him from freezing. The bird was upset and distraught because it couldn't understand why, at his lowest point in life, the cow would want to #2 on him and make his situation worse.

Finally, a fox came along and saw this poor bird, crippled, helpless, and covered in excrement. He scrambled into the ditch and rescued the bird. He then took the bird to the river and gave him a bath. The bird was extremely happy and grateful that he had finally found a friend who could help him. The fox then ate the bird because his only motive for doing all of those nice things was so that he could have a meal. So, as my dad says, "The moral of the story, darlin', is that everyone who shi*s on you is not your enemy and everyone who lends a helping hand is definitely *not* your friend."

As someone who is making boss moves, it is important that you guard whatever it is that you are trying to build. Everyone can't come along on this journey with you. You have to be discerning about who it is that you allow into your inner circle and their motivation for helping you.

At the same time, there will also be people who appear to be against you and that's okay too. Just shake it off and find any life lesson that you can in the circumstance. If someone takes advantage of you, thank them for making you wiser. If they are discouraging, thank them for making you stronger and more determined. Most importantly, keep it moving. At the end of the day, with all of the games that we play in each other's lives, don't let the actions of others change your character and goodness of heart. Most people are filled with good intentions, and the general rule is that what you put out into the world will come back to you.

Failure Is Inevitable

I've missed more than 9000 shots in my career. I've lost almost 300 games. 26 times, I've been trusted to take the game winning shot and missed. I've failed over and over and over again in my life. And that is why I succeed.
– Michael Jordon

I'm not going to sugarcoat this. Successful people fail and they fail a lot! It is simply a part of the process and it hurts! Even with our best efforts and doing everything we know how to do, we will still experience failure and that's okay as long as you get up and keep trying.

We have been taught from childhood that failing is bad, but no one ever teaches us that failing is inevitable. Thus, throughout our lives, when we encounter failure we tend to take it personally. I know I did.

I, too, have had some pretty epic failures in my life. I have experienced failures in school, relationships, jobs, diets, business, and I could go on and on. Some of these failures have taken me to the lowest points of my life where I even questioned whether or not life was worth living. I don't want anyone to ever have to experience that if they don't have to because a lot of people tend to get stuck there and it is all due not truly understanding failure and the opportunity that it provides.

When people commit suicide, they often leave notes. As a part of my job, I read those notes and they often take me back to a place where I once found myself. It was a place where an epic failure actually turned out to be one of the biggest blessings of my life although I was unable to see it at the time. I couldn't see that by overcoming this so-called failure, I would be able to influence and impact other people. I couldn't see that because of this failure I would meet many people who I would not trade for the world because of how they helped me to overcome it. I couldn't see that I would emerge stronger, wiser, and much happier on the other side. All I could see was that I failed and that I was worthless as a person (which I realize is untrue, but that is how I felt at the time). That is the absolute wrong way to look at failure.

The great news is that none of us are alone in experiencing failure. It is said that someone once asked Thomas Edison how it felt to fail five thousand times before discovering the electric light bulb. His answer was that he did not fail five thousand times; instead, he successfully discovered five thousand ways that it did not work. He had the ability to see his failures simply as stepping stones rather than insurmountable obstacles. He did not take them personally as they were merely objective results in his mind. This enabled him to stay focused on his goal and continue to take consistent action.

People who focus on "failure" in this way are able to find the valuable lessons in every setback and they attempt to fail as often and as quickly as possible. They don't focus on the problem or the loss. They make their problems work for them and instead of being fixated on what they did wrong, they focus on what they did right and how they can do it differently next time. They focus on learning new things that will lead to success.

An outcome of failure is an event, not a person. It is a temporary detour and often occurs as a result of trying something new. Never let a failure make you feel as if you are inferior or unworthy. It only says that you are not perfect—none of us are. We can't stop failures and setbacks from appearing in our lives, but we can control how we choose to handle them. There is no significant meaning in failure other than to get back up and keep trying.

LEGACY

Success is not about how much money you make, it is about the difference you make in other people's lives.
– **Michelle Obama**

Live in Order to Leave a Legacy of Love

Legacy is not what's left tomorrow when you are gone. It is what you give, create, impact, and contribute today while you are here that then happens to live on.
– Rasheed Ogunlaru

The only things in life that you can truly call your own are the results of your own actions. They will be your legacy in this world and will outlive you long after you have left this earth. What you did, how you lived, and whose lives you were able to touch along the way are the cornerstones of legacy. I am sure we all have huge and pressing "To Do" lists that take up a lot of our attention, but how many of us are focusing on how we want "To Be" in life? In essence, what would you like to leave behind? What are the principles that you would like to champion? In all that you do, there should also be a message of how you would like to be remembered as well.

We currently have the opportunity to make this time in our history and culture one of the greatest for healing, transformation, and growth. In order to do this, we need determined people with huge and open hearts who want to make an impact in this world. We need people who are successful, happy, and fulfilled—people who can pour out their knowledge and wisdom into our future generations.

Imagine our communities filled with people who radiate self-love, love and acceptance for others, empowerment, and abundance. Imagine our communities if these same people are willing and able to pass these traits down to their children and to the children of the world around them so that fewer people are subject to living lives of despair and disempowerment regardless of their ethnicity, sexuality, or religion.

People have seen and heard of the astronomical gun violence that occurs in cities like Chicago, yet no one hardly says a word unless it is in the spirit of criticism or contempt. This isn't something you can "fight." There has to be another option. One where those who aren't affected on a direct level acknowledge the devastation and truly see, hear, and feel for those who are. We must see the senseless loss of lives, hear the soul-wrenching cries of those left behind, and feel their pain as if it were one of our own family members *because it is*. These things aren't happening in a matrix or in a video game! These are *real* people and too many *real and valuable* lives are being cut short every single day. Dr. Martin Luther King Jr said that "an injustice anywhere is a threat to justice everywhere" and if he were here today, my bet is that he would agree that this applies regardless of who is pulling the trigger.

When people look back on this time in history, a time when people are desperate and hurting and when black lives don't really *feel* as if they matter very much, I want them to see a people who took their hurt, pain, and in certain cases, their privilege and transmuted it into something positive for generations to come. I want us to create a community of people who, in their brokenness, made the decision to heal, love, and not let their destinies be deterred by the hateful actions of a small sect of people, stuck in the quicksand of ignorance and hate, who have internalized the hate spewed by the media. I want each individual to take a stand and if nothing else, make a personal decision that their life as an individual does matter.

I would like to see communities and individuals choose paths that lead to success and noteworthy contributions for the human family. I yearn to see the day when we, as humans, reach our full potential as a society, but we are not going to be able to do so if we don't respect one another based solely on simple, petty things like race or income level. If you subscribe to any theology of the God of Abraham, He has basically given us two essential rules to live by: #1. Love God and #2. Love each other as you love your own self.

So while this book has provided a blue print of how people of African-American heritage can still find their destiny in these turbulent times, the burden is certainly not ours alone to carry. We simply can't. Every life that is lost prematurely and/or without warrant affects each and every person in this country whether they would like to admit it or not. It affects future generations and the world they will live in.

Hate, rage, and anger that stews, festers, and is passed down to the next generation of leaders, and possibly revolutionaries, is never a good thing. My father served as a police officer for over twenty years and I can remember him telling me that the scariest man alive is the one who feels like he has *nothing* left to lose. Feigned ignorance of these issues is dangerous and I personally do not want to live in a world where an entire generation of kids and men feel as if they are not valued, not seen, not heard, not loved, not protected, and not given justice. In turn, because of this, they have *nothing* in this world left to lose.

As I reflect upon the 100th monkey and its connection to the issues of the day, I think about the eloquent words of Dr. Martin Luther King Jr's "I Have a Dream" speech in 1963. As if immortalized in a time capsule, his words still ring true today: "Now is the time to make justice a reality for *all* of God's children. It would be *fatal* for the nation to overlook the urgency of the moment...the marvelous new militancy which has engulfed the Negro community must not lead us to distrust all white people, for many of our white brothers, as evidenced by their presence here today, have come to realize that their destiny is tied up with our destiny. They have come to realize that their freedom is inextricably bound to our freedom. We cannot walk alone, and as we walk we must pledge that we will always march ahead. We cannot turn back."

It is easy to read these words as mere rhetorical genius, but in doing so, we neglect to honor our divine connection as members of humanity. Recently, when I have turned on the news or scrolled through my Facebook newsfeed, I have had to pause to look at the calendar just to make sure that I am still in the year 2018. Some days I feel as though I have been teleported back in time to when the air was palpably vile and vitreous. Some days, I feel like I have been transported into a war zone where I am on the losing side. Then I realize that we are merely at one of those critical forks in the road on the timeline of humanity and the question becomes: Who will you decide to become during these turbulent times? What will you contribute to the legacy of humanity?

I urge you to ponder carefully as your answer will affect us all. Will you be the one who shows up and leaves a better legacy for our children? Will you be the one who helps wash away the dirt of society so life can be better for others?

Surely, if a monkey can figure out a better way, so can we as humans.

Love, success, and purpose always,
Dr. LaTanja Watkins, MD

If you would like to dive deeper into the concepts of this book and start getting ahead even faster, go to

www.hundredthnubian.com

to download your FREE workbook.